words of
courage
for
Women

words of courage *for* Women

Carolyn Larsen

Revell

a division of Baker Publishing Group
Grand Rapids, Michigan

Published by Revell
a division of Baker Publishing Group
PO Box 6287, Grand Rapids, MI 49516-6287
www.revellbooks.com

Printed in the United States of America

Library of Congress Cataloging-in-Publication Data
Names: Larsen, Carolyn, 1950– author.
Title: Words of courage for women / Carolyn Larsen.
Description: Grand Rapids : Revell, a division of Baker Publishing Group, 2020.
Identifiers: LCCN 2019028426 | ISBN 9780800736446
Subjects: LCSH: Christian women—Religious life—Meditations. | Courage—
    Religious aspects—Christianity—Meditations.
Classification: LCC BV4527 .L3445 2020 | DDC 242/.643—dc23
LC record available at https://lccn.loc.gov/2019028426

20   21   22   23   24   25   26   7   6   5   4   3   2   1

The Source of Courage

Surely God is my salvation;
  I will trust and not be afraid.
The LORD, the LORD himself, is my strength and my
  defense;
  he has become my salvation.

ISAIAH 12:2

Why does fear take root in your heart? Are you afraid you can't withstand temptations or that you won't be able to stand against Satan's attacks? When you invite Jesus into your heart, he becomes your strength to stand against all frightening things. He becomes your shield against danger and your defender against all enemies.

God promises in his Word to always be with you. Read that again: *always!* He's the source of your courage. Allow his strength to fill your heart so you can face whatever is before you. Never doubt his power because, after all, he promised it to you.

What can you do when anxiety threatens to paralyze your heart? Push the fear away by focusing on God. Read Scripture. Remind yourself of how he has strengthened and protected you in the past, and remind yourself that his powerful presence is still with you. Step confidently into your day, and refuse to cower in fear.

Start each day by renewing your courage through the quietness of prayer and through rest in God. Ask him to fill your heart with an awareness of his power and presence and to bolster your courage through that knowledge.

2

Perfect Love

There is no fear in love. But perfect love drives out fear, because fear has to do with punishment. The one who fears is not made perfect in love.

1 JOHN 4:18

Fear is an interesting emotion. Even when you try to have courage, fear wiggles its way into your heart, similar to the way water manages to leak through the smallest opening. A little anxiety is certainly normal because life does have its tense moments and . . . you're human. However, all-consuming fear and trust in God's love cannot exist in your heart at the same time. If you truly believe that God loves you, why are you afraid?

God's love is perfect. What does that mean to you? Perfect love is deep, pure, constant, steady, forgiving, trustworthy, dependable, protective, sacrificial, and a multitude of other adjectives. Perfect love . . . there is nothing wrong with it and nothing to criticize about it. Grasping, believing, and trusting in God's perfect love for you helps push away fear because you know God is protecting you and guiding your decisions and steps. He loves you perfectly, so there is no reason to fear. Take courage in his love. Ask God to help your love for him grow deeper so that you have a greater understanding of his care for you.

3

Guarded

You hem me in behind and before,
and you lay your hand upon me.

PSALM 139:5

You've probably seen photos of celebrities out in public, surrounded by security guards they've hired to protect them. They have a wall of guards around them to make certain no one gets too close. The guards protect their employer on all sides and constantly evaluate the crowd for any situation that might bring danger to them.

Maybe you can't afford to hire bodyguards to protect you wherever you go. But here's some news: you have the best bodyguard imaginable—God! The psalmist says God is in front of you and behind you. Nothing and no one gets close to you without God knowing about it. And not only is he protecting you in front and in back, but he also has his hand on your shoulder, guiding your steps and making sure you don't fall, much like a loving parent who helps a child cross a busy street.

It is amazing to know that God loves you so much that he protects you, guards you, and guides you. He cares about what happens to you every moment of the day. When anxiety begins to rear its ugly head, remember that you are well guarded. Trust your Bodyguard!

4

The Love of a Father

The Spirit you received does not make you slaves, so that you live in fear again; rather, the Spirit you received brought about your adoption to sonship. And by him we cry, "Abba, Father."

ROMANS 8:15

Not every human father is a good father, and if you haven't had a good father, that may influence how you perceive God as Father. If that's true for you, read the following description of God as your good Father:

> Your good Father wants the best for you. Yes, sometimes that may mean he disciplines you because that's what a good father does in order to help you learn and grow.
>
> Your good Father watches out for you. He does all he can to protect you, day in and day out.
>
> Your good Father delights in you. He enjoys your laughter. He takes pleasure in your enjoyment of all he

provides for you, from the world he has made to the friends and family he has given you. Enjoy it all!

Your good Father is forgiving. Don't be afraid to confess your sins to him. He won't turn away in disgust. He won't turn away at all. He forgives you and offers a multitude of opportunities for you to get life right, even as he teaches and guides you.

You needn't ever be afraid of your good Father; in fact, you can be brave and courageous in the knowledge that you are your Father's child and that he loves you more than you can imagine.

5

Just for This Time

> *If you remain silent at this time, relief and deliverance for the Jews will arise from another place, but you and your father's family will perish. And who knows but that you have come to your royal position for such a time as this?*
>
> ESTHER 4:14

It takes courage to tackle some of the challenges that come your way in life. Some of those challenges arise from tasks God calls you to handle. Has God given you a job that feels too big or too dangerous or even beyond what you have the capability to accomplish?

Queen Esther felt that way. The task before her was very dangerous. She could have been killed for doing what she was asked to do. If she was successful, she would save the Jewish nation. If she wasn't, they would die and so would she.

What can you learn from Esther? She accepted the challenge but asked her people to pray for her. She didn't go into the challenge without their prayer support. Esther accepted the reality that facing this challenge might have been the very reason God put her on earth: "For such a time as this."

God has a purpose for your life—work he wants you to do for his kingdom. He won't send you into that work without walking beside you and equipping you with what you need. The prayer support of others certainly strengthens you too. You aren't alone, so be courageous and go boldly into what God calls you to do.

6

The Hardest Thing

Wait for the LORD;
be strong and take heart
and wait for the LORD.
PSALM 27:14

Are you familiar with the expression "like a bull in a china shop"? It's a description of someone who rushes into situations without thinking things through, without preparing adequately, or without having all the information. Rushing into anything in this manner seldom ends well.

When a crisis arises in your life or when a difficult situation is in front of you, is it your tendency to rush in and try to handle things yourself, without God's guidance or power? Sure, you pray, but if God doesn't move or direct you quickly enough—well, waiting is hard. In fact, one of the most difficult things God may ever ask you to do is . . . wait.

It takes courage to wait for God. But waiting means you trust him. It shows that you believe he will either handle the situation or give you wisdom and direction to know what to do. Even if the crisis goes on for a long time, you wait because you trust him.

Do you want to know how courageous you are? Do you want to test how strong your faith is? Then wait on God's guidance, and wait on his action.

7

Courage to Face Temptation

No temptation has overtaken you except what is common to mankind. And God is faithful; he will not let you be tempted beyond what you can bear. But when you are tempted, he will also provide a way out so that you can endure it.

1 Corinthians 10:13

Temptation is a part of life. Certainly not a pleasant part, but still a part. There may be certain temptations that cause you to be especially anxious because you know they are hard for you to resist. But here's the thing: there is no temptation you face that hasn't been faced by others in the past or that won't be faced by people in the future. And you won't face any temptations that God doesn't already know about. He knows absolutely everything that comes into your life.

What can you do to be able to look temptation in the face and not be afraid? How can you have the assurance that you will be able to withstand temptation? The best thing to do is to ask God for help. Ask him for strength, wisdom, and guidance. Then pay attention to how he answers your prayer. Don't expect him to take the temptation away, because he knows your faith in him will grow stronger as you trust his strength to help you stand up to the temptation. Through his help, you will find the courage to face the temptation, and your faith will grow stronger and deeper because of it.

8

God's Restoration

The God of all grace, who called you to his eternal glory in Christ, after you have suffered a little while, will himself restore you and make you strong, firm and steadfast.

1 PETER 5:10

You will undoubtedly experience problems at one time or another in your life. But, instead of being discouraged by them, remember that these things can serve to make you stronger. Search the words of Scripture to be reminded of God's presence and care for you. Focus on the lessons you're learning and how your dependence on God is growing stronger because of your experiences. It's true that there are struggles in life and that you have an enemy trying to pull you away from God.

But have courage! You're not in the battle against Satan by yourself. God is paying attention and is ready to strengthen and protect you. Call on him to help you get through your troubles. He wants to help your faith grow stronger and deeper. When you experience his power and restoration after you've struggled and suffered, your trust will grow deeper. Then you can face with courage any problems that come, because you know God is with you and he won't let the troubles you face destroy you. So go forward with courage. See God's hand in your life. Trust him to be there for you!

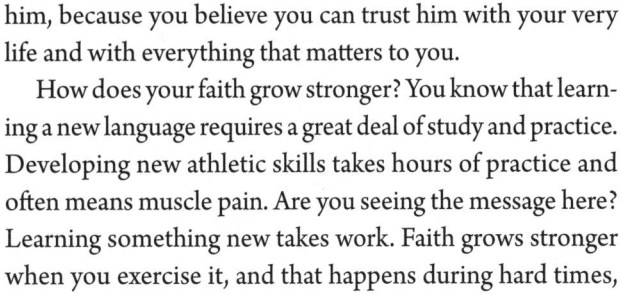

9

What's Your Goal?

Consider it pure joy, my brothers and sisters, whenever you face trials of many kinds, because you know that the testing of your faith produces perseverance. Let perseverance finish its work so that you may be mature and complete, not lacking anything.

JAMES 1:2–4

When you invite Jesus into your heart, you become a child of God. Great, but that's not the end of the story. You want your faith to grow stronger and deeper. You want to know God more intimately and become more dependent on him, because you believe you can trust him with your very life and with everything that matters to you.

How does your faith grow stronger? You know that learning a new language requires a great deal of study and practice. Developing new athletic skills takes hours of practice and often means muscle pain. Are you seeing the message here? Learning something new takes work. Faith grows stronger when you exercise it, and that happens during hard times, when your faith is tested. Is it fun or easy? No, of course not. But when you face problems and trust God to help you through them, you are persevering. So commit to staying close to him, leaning on him, and letting him guide you through your problems. As you see him leading, strengthening, and guiding, your faith muscle will grow stronger because you will know he is always with you and you can trust him no matter what. And with that trust, as James encourages, you may become mature and complete, lacking nothing!

10

Peace and Courage

*You will keep in perfect peace
those whose minds are steadfast,
because they trust in you.*

ISAIAH 26:3

Your thought life can take you on some interesting journeys if you let it. It will take you on the "What if this happens?" journey and the "Why didn't I do this or say that?" trip. If you depend on your thought life to be a trip advisor or a planning tool, things will seldom turn out well. Peace will not be the outcome.

However, there is a way for peace to be the foundation of your life.

Keep your thoughts settled on God. Make him and his Word the filter that all other thoughts pass through. When anxiety and fear start to wiggle into your thoughts, stop and pray. Read God's Word. Focus on Bible verses that remind you of God's presence and his immense love for you. Remind yourself of ways he has protected you and guided you in the past. Refuse to let the what-if thoughts take control of your mind. Allow your trust in God to push them away. Remember the many times he has shown you how very much he loves you and has proven that he will take care of you.

Keeping your thoughts locked on God because you know that you can trust him gives you courage to face whatever life brings. It also gives you peace as you go through difficult times.

11

World-Changing Courage

> *When they saw him walking on the lake, they thought he was a ghost. They cried out, because they all saw him and were terrified.*
>
> *Immediately he spoke to them and said, "Take courage! It is I. Don't be afraid."*
>
> MARK 6:49–50

What's your reaction when God does something incredibly amazing? How do you feel when you see the majesty of his creativity and strength in nature? Are you a little frightened at his power and greatness? (The disciples were.) Does the scope of his might that's available in your life entice or frighten you?

When you come face-to-face with the power of Jesus through circumstances, through nature, through your own heart, don't be terrified. Instead, let that experience make you aware of the infinite power available to you through your relationship with him. His power will change you, change lives, change the world. Are you ready for that? The disciples were terrified because, when they saw him walking on top of the water, they didn't know what to think about his control.

Jesus told them, "Take courage! It is I. Don't be afraid." Hear him say that to you, and let the possibilities of his power in your life give you courage to exercise a risk-taking faith that will be used mightily by God!

12

Courage to Love Others

Love your enemies and pray for those who persecute you, that you may be children of your Father in heaven. He causes his sun to rise on the evil and the good, and sends rain on the righteous and the unrighteous.

MATTHEW 5:44–45

At some point in your life, someone may become upset with you. You may even have an enemy because of someone's perceptions of you or because of something you've said or done. How do you respond to someone who is upset with you? Do you get angry in response? Do you bad-mouth that person? Do you try to get others on your side of the situation? Or do you love . . . just love?

It takes courage to love someone who doesn't love you back. It takes courage to even be kind to someone who may not receive that kindness well. But you must remember whose child you are. Your powerful heavenly Father will give you the courage to speak a word of kindness. He will give you the strength to lift your hand—not so you can strike out at the other person, but so you can shake their hand, give them a pat on the back, or even give them a gentle hug.

Yes, loving those who don't like you is hard. It means taking a risk, so it takes courage. That courage comes from the powerful love of God in your heart. Ask him to help you love your enemies. He will fill your heart with courage.

13

Courage to Heal Relationships

Do not repay anyone evil for evil. Be careful to do what is right in the eyes of everyone. If it is possible, as far as it depends on you, live at peace with everyone.

ROMANS 12:17–18

Relationships are wonderful. Families, spouses, friends—life would be pretty boring without them. But once in a while stress creeps into your relationships, which may cause you to react or respond in a way that isn't the best. It takes courage to admit when you haven't behaved your best. When you have an issue with another person, the temptation is to be self-protective or even to get a little revenge. But that's not the way to emulate God's love to others, is it? Keep in the forefront of your thoughts that your responsibility is first and foremost to be an ambassador of Jesus Christ by your words, attitudes, and behaviors.

Step forward with courage and admit your personal failure in the situation. Ask forgiveness. Reestablish communication. Make it your goal, as the apostle Paul instructs, to live at peace with others. It will not always be easy. It will sometimes mean sacrificing your feelings and living humbly. When you need help to do this, ask God for strength and to help you see situations from a viewpoint other than your own.

14

Courage to Share Your Faith

Jesus came to them and said, "All authority in heaven and on earth has been given to me. Therefore go and make disciples of all nations, baptizing them in the name of the Father and of the Son and of the Holy Spirit, and teaching them to obey everything I have commanded you. And surely I am with you always, to the very end of the age."

MATTHEW 28:18–20

Before he went back to heaven, Jesus instructed his followers to tell others about God's love. Do you find it scary to speak about your faith to another person? Do you have trouble finding the right words? Are you nervous that people will reject your message—or that they'll even reject you?

The news of God's love is the best news ever, but it takes courage and sensitivity to share it with others. If you don't share your faith, people you care about may miss out on the best news ever given and the blessing of knowing God. That means they could miss the blessing of eternity in heaven. This is serious, so you must believe the importance of your message. If you need courage to share your faith, ask God to help you share his love with those he brings into your life. He will give you opportunities, the right words, and a deep passion to share his love. Your courage should come from the last part of these verses in Matthew: You're not on your own to share your faith—Jesus is with you. Always.

15

Focused on God

Look to the LORD and his strength;
seek his face always.
1 CHRONICLES 16:11

When you're afraid, where do you turn for help? Do you turn within? To friends? To power? To money? To success? Wherever you turn indicates what you feel is most likely to calm your fear. It shows where you're putting your trust. Where is the focus of your heart and mind?

When you need strength and courage, the only solution that offers true hope is God. His strength is without measure. His power is beyond comprehension. The ocean waves obey him. Weather obeys him. He is the Creator of everything, and his power is greater than anything else on earth.

Whatever help you need, whatever part of your life in which you are struggling with waning strength, God is the answer. Put your trust in him to guide you and help you with any challenges life brings your way. Keep your heart always turned toward him. Don't let anything push God out of the number one position in your heart and thoughts. Other things will constantly try to usurp his position, but be careful that nothing becomes more important than God's love and approval in your life. Your faith will grow stronger and deeper as you see you can trust him in every aspect of your life.

Love Song

The Lord your God is with you,
the Mighty Warrior who saves.
He will take great delight in you;
in his love he will no longer rebuke you,
but will rejoice over you with singing.

ZEPHANIAH 3:17

God is with you. Nothing will happen to you today that he doesn't already know about. He will walk with you through whatever difficult, frightening experiences come along.

It's safe to say that God saves you multiple times even in one day because he's watching over you. He keeps your foot from a false step; he stops your car in time to prevent an accident. Does he stop every single crisis? No, but he gives his presence so you're never alone.

God doesn't just save you, he celebrates you. It gives him joy to be with you, to give you things, and to do things for you. Think about that—the Creator of everything in the universe actually delights in having you close to him.

He forgives the sins you commit and the times you push him to the background. Accept his forgiveness, and also forgive yourself and move forward in your life with him.

Lastly, realize that God himself is singing a love song over you, for you, because of you. So be courageous in your walk with him. Love him with abandon because that's how he loves you!

17

Courage When You're Discouraged

My dear brothers and sisters, stand firm. Let nothing move you. Always give yourselves fully to the work of the Lord, because you know that your labor in the Lord is not in vain.

1 CORINTHIANS 15:58

Having courage means being brave, having nerve, being daring. There's strength in the word *courage*. The word *discouraged*, while it has the same root word, means downcast, disheartened, and dejected. There's weakness in this word.

You may get discouraged when you're doing God's work—whether that means parenting as a Christ follower, living a godly example before an unbelieving spouse, being a Christian employee, or serving as a professional in Christian ministry. You may sometimes feel as though you're failing, or you may get discouraged because you see no progress. It can be hard to persevere.

Trust the apostle Paul's words here so you don't get discouraged. Nothing you do for the Lord is ever in vain. While it's true that you may not see the positive results of your efforts for a long time (or even in your lifetime), you can trust that your work is laying a foundation in someone's life. Someone else may add the next layer for that person, but be assured that every word you spoke, every helping hand you offered, every prayer you prayed will be used by the Lord. So keep serving with love and intentionality. Have courage in sharing your faith and in doing God's work because he *will* use everything you do for his kingdom!

Be Prepared

*Put on the full armor of God, so that you can take your stand
against the devil's schemes.*

EPHESIANS 6:11

What are you struggling with? Relationship issues? Too many commitments? Parenting? Temptation? How are you going to win these battles? They might look like normal, everyday battles, but they are attacks by Satan to pull you away from God. That's his goal. But God has provided all the protection you need to fight off Satan's attacks. The protection is there. You just have to use it.

Putting on the armor of God takes an intentional effort on your part. He has provided it, but you must take action. Some pieces of the armor may be difficult to put on and practice faithfully—for example, the one that covers your thought life and choices. Satan plants thoughts that make you doubt God's care, thoughts that lead to judgment and criticism of others, and thoughts that make you question your self-worth. You know where your weakest point is, so concentrate on preparing yourself for battle by putting on that piece of armor.

Once you have prepared yourself for life by putting on the armor of God outlined in Ephesians 6—the truth of who God is, righteousness, readiness, faith, and salvation—you will be prepared and protected by what God has provided, and you can courageously and powerfully face whatever life brings.

19

Courage While Waiting

They will have no fear of bad news;
their hearts are steadfast, trusting in the LORD.
PSALM 112:7

When you undergo medical tests, you must then wait for the results. The waiting is the hardest part. You're in a holding pattern. You try to keep your mind away from what the results might be. You try not to think about the what-if questions. You try to have courageous faith.

It's okay to be afraid. Whether you're awaiting the results of a medical test or you're dealing with another issue, the road ahead is unknown and it very well may not be easy. However, you can certainly trust that nothing will happen to you without God knowing about it first. You can know that your trust in him will take you to a deeper, more trusting faith, and that kind of growth comes only through trial and testing. Whatever your test results may be, you will not have to go through even one second of the journey alone. God is walking with you, holding you close, loving you, and teaching you every step of the way. Find courage in a deeper, more intimate relationship with him. Let his courage fill your heart.

Uniquely You

There are different kinds of gifts, but the same Spirit distributes them. There are different kinds of service, but the same Lord. There are different kinds of working, but in all of them and in everyone it is the same God at work.

1 Corinthians 12:4–6

Do you ever feel boxed in by others' opinions or expectations of you? People can pigeonhole you to be a certain way, to behave a certain way, and even to serve God in a certain way. Once you've slid into a certain niche and stayed there for a while, it might be scary to try something new. Sometimes that's fine. But what if God wants you to try something new? Are you courageous enough to step into that?

God has given you certain gifts to use in certain ways to serve him. Don't get caught up in doing what you've always done if he is nudging you to do something new. Don't look at someone else and wish you could be just like them. Be courageous enough to be the real you and to serve God and others through that realness. God will work through you to accomplish whatever he calls you to do. Look for the adventure of the new and unique. Be willing to try new things, and see where God leads you!

21

Taking On the Big Guy

David said to the Philistine, "You come against me with sword and spear and javelin, but I come against you in the name of the LORD Almighty, the God of the armies of Israel, whom you have defied."

1 SAMUEL 17:45

You may know the story of young David rising to the challenge of a giant named Goliath who was armed with a shield and spear, while David had only a slingshot and a few stones. David wasn't afraid. He knew he could win. God was on his side, so he knew he could defeat the big, powerful, well-trained giant. He was right. Nothing and no one is stronger than God.

What "Goliath" are you facing in your life? A job change? Relationship struggles? Health issues? Finding your way in life? Changes in your life situation are challenges for sure. It takes courage to face them and keep moving forward. Where does that courage come from? God himself. Remember that the Lord Almighty is fighting for you. Stop and think about his power displayed in creation and his control over the wind, rain, ocean, and all of nature. Think about how God interacted with his people in Scripture—especially in the Old Testament. His power is immeasurable. His strength is unmatched. His love for you is unconditional. Take courage to face whatever your Goliath might be, because the Lord Almighty, the God of the armies of Israel, is fighting for you!

Courage in the Dark

> Even though I walk
>   through the darkest valley,
> I will fear no evil,
>   for you are with me;
> your rod and your staff,
>   they comfort me.
>
> PSALM 23:4

When children are afraid, they want to be close to someone they trust, someone they know will take care of and protect them. They feel safe when they're with certain people, and they gain courage from that closeness. Any monsters or bad guys they might perceive to be in the darkness are minimized by the presence of someone they trust to protect them.

You have an even more powerful bodyguard walking through life with you: God. Life may take you through some very dark valleys with tall cliffs on either side that hide the sunlight. But the thing is, you don't walk through those valleys alone. Your loving Father goes before you and follows after you. He guides your every step, even when you can't see solid ground ahead of you. He protects you from anything that could sneak up from behind to destroy you. He comforts you in the pain of the journey. He whispers to your heart, "You can do it. You can make it. Keep going." He cares about what you're going through. Knowing he's with you gives you courage to keep moving forward one step at a time.

23

The Rubber Meets the Road

Do not let your hearts be troubled. You believe in God; believe also in me.

JOHN 14:1

If you've accepted Jesus as your Savior, then you have confessed that you believe he is truly the Messiah, God's Son. You believe that he was present at the creation of all there is. You believe his power, strength, and wisdom are greater than any other power, strength, and wisdom.

But where the rubber meets the road—in other words, where the honesty and depth of your faith come into play—is at a point in your life when you face a crisis that sends you into a spiral of fear and worry. How you react to troubles shows your true opinion and feelings about your faith.

Jesus says that if you truly believe in him, you can trust his power, strength, wisdom, and love. Complete trust that leads to powerful courage is the goal. Does this happen easily? Not necessarily. But each time you push fear aside, trust him, and see his response, your faith grows stronger. Each time you cry out to Jesus for help, your belief deepens. Faith is a journey. Learn from each experience, and your courage will deepen as your fear fades away in the realization and experience of Jesus's love and power.

24

Take a Risk

When she heard about Jesus, she came up behind him in the crowd and touched his cloak, because she thought, "If I just touch his clothes, I will be healed." Immediately her bleeding stopped and she felt in her body that she was freed from her suffering.

MARK 5:27–29

This woman's story is told in just a few verses in three of the Gospels. She suffered from a bleeding issue for twelve years. She spent all her money on doctors, to no avail. Her condition made her unclean, which may have kept other people away from her so they wouldn't become unclean too. She could have given up, but she didn't. She took a chance by going into a crowd of people following Jesus. She pushed her way past people who wouldn't have wanted her to touch them. Why did she do this? Because she believed that if she could just touch Jesus's clothes, she would be healed. That would be enough. It was.

How courageous is your faith? Are you willing to push your way through people or situations that are difficult in order to get closer to Jesus? Do you believe that Jesus's power is so strong that (figuratively) touching his clothes by keeping your heart focused on him and choosing to trust him no matter what will get a response? Remember what Jesus said to this woman: "Daughter, your faith has healed you. Go in peace and be freed from your suffering" (v. 34). Have a courageous faith!

25

Courage to Forgive

Bear with each other and forgive one another if any of you has a grievance against someone. Forgive as the Lord forgave you.

COLOSSIANS 3:13

Forgiving when you've been wronged—intentionally or unintentionally—is hard, especially if the person who hurt you doesn't apologize or show some repentance. In this situation, forgiving means pushing aside your own feelings and allowing God to help you forgive and to mean it. This is when forgiving takes courage.

Remember that whoever hurt you is just a person . . . as you are . . . and you know that you sometimes make mistakes, that you're sometimes selfish, that you sometimes simply do not pay attention to how your words or actions impact someone else.

Remember, too, that your anger is holding you prisoner. The energy it takes to stay angry is hurting only you. Forgiveness frees your heart to love and give and enjoy.

Where does God come into this? You will need his strength working in your heart to help you forgive. Let go of your anger. Let go of your self-centered focus, and let God help you forgive. Remember that he forgives you over and over for your shortcomings and failures. He does so willingly and lovingly. Let him give you the courage to extend forgiveness to others. In doing that, you will find freedom from your anger.

26

Courage to Walk Away

The LORD is my light and my salvation—
whom shall I fear?
The LORD is the stronghold of my life—
of whom shall I be afraid?

PSALM 27:1

Sometimes people come into your life who seem to be good for you; however, eventually you see that particular relationship is not healthy for you. Perhaps the interactions with this person are damaging to your self-esteem. Or, even more serious, they could be damaging to your relationship with God. It will take courage to step away from this person. It can be frightening. Where do you get the courage? It comes from knowing that God is on your side. He loves you very much, and his desire is for your relationship with him to grow deeper and deeper. So if someone is intentionally or selfishly pulling you away from God, he will help you walk away from them. He will give you the courage and the wisdom to do so with kindness. And he will protect you in the process, so you have nothing to fear.

Choose God and make him your stronghold—a place that is fortified to protect those inside it from attack. When you are covered with God's protection, there's nothing to fear because he will not let anything or anyone get to you. Your courage comes from your trust that God will protect you and care for you.

Courage to Let Go

Offer your bodies as a living sacrifice, holy and pleasing to God—this is your true and proper worship. Do not conform to the pattern of this world, but be transformed by the renewing of your mind. Then you will be able to test and approve what God's will is—his good, pleasing and perfect will.

ROMANS 12:1–2

Most people have at least an idea of a plan for their life. But what if your hopes, dreams, and goals aren't what God has planned for you? It's hard to give up control of your own life, even when you know you can trust the One you submit that control to. God asks you to offer yourself to him, lock, stock, and barrel—holding nothing back. The apostle Paul says to do so is actually your worship of God. Why does he say that? Possibly because having the courage to let go of your own agenda and desires and submitting to what God has for you shows that you trust him completely and you honor his wisdom, strength, and omniscience.

Separating yourself from what the world says is important makes room in your heart and mind for God to shift your thoughts and desires to what he knows is truly important.

Do you trust God enough to let go of your life and follow his guiding and will for you? He has only your best interests at heart, which, of course, include the ways you serve him and others. Trust him enough to let go and follow him.

Courage to Ask

If any of you lacks wisdom, you should ask God, who gives generously to all without finding fault, and it will be given to you.

JAMES 1:5

You don't have to have all the answers for everything in life. It's okay to ask for help, especially from God. However, for some of us it's hard to ask for help or advice. In our pride, we want to believe we always know what to do and how to think. But life isn't that easy, so sometimes we need help from the One who has true wisdom.

God won't think any less of you for asking for help; in fact, he will appreciate your questions because they show your dependence on him and your recognition of his wisdom. The hardest part of asking for help is admitting that you need the help. Courageously put your pride aside, submit to the truth of God's omniscience, and ask him to help you form your thoughts, speak the right words, and make good decisions. He will guide your thoughts and words to reflect his own heart if you will let him. Just ask; he's waiting to help you.

29

Courage to Grieve

> The LORD is close to the brokenhearted
> and saves those who are crushed in spirit.
>
> PSALM 34:18

Losing someone you love is so crushing that your heart feels deeply bruised. Any reminder of that loved one brings grief rolling to the surface. Grief is real and it can be consuming, but it's important to go through the grieving process.

Experiencing grief doesn't mean you're weak, and it doesn't mean you don't trust God or believe he will comfort your soul. It may take courage to admit you are grieving. Ask him to give you that courage so he can touch your heart, walk with you through the grief journey, and bring you through it.

God cares about your pain and loss because he loves you. So turn to him when your heart is aching, and let him remind you of the promise of eternity with your loved one. He will bring other people near to remind you that others need your presence in their lives and that you matter to them. God will give you purpose in your life and reasons to get up and be active each day. Let your loving Father come close to you so he can comfort your grieving heart.

30

Courage to Not Judge

When they kept on questioning him, he straightened up and said to them, "Let any one of you who is without sin be the first to throw a stone at her."

JOHN 8:7

It's tempting to appoint yourself judge over other people, to decide the motives for what they do or say, or to assign the reasons for how they've behaved. Some people leap to the judgment of others without even having all the information surrounding their actions or knowing the full story of a situation. A person can get pretty arrogant about their own righteousness when they've become the judge of others.

You show courage when you admit that you've thought, said, and done wrong things as much as anyone else has. Your courage guides you to push away the temptation to judge others or view them negatively.

It takes courage to offer grace to others, especially those who seem to have no repentance or regret for what they've done. So you must ask your loving, grace-giving heavenly Father to help you remember your own sin and to fill you with forgiveness and grace toward all. Leave the work of judging others exactly where it belongs—with God. Take care of your own heart by asking God to forgive your sins and to fill you with generous compassion.

31

Fueled by Love

I am convinced that neither death nor life, neither angels nor demons, neither the present nor the future, nor any powers, neither height nor depth, nor anything else in all creation, will be able to separate us from the love of God that is in Christ Jesus our Lord.

ROMANS 8:38–39

Are you afraid of failing God? You know you're a sinner who breaks God's commands. But are you anxious about admitting that to him because you fear he will turn away from you? He won't. Nothing can separate you from God's love—not even your own sin. He loves you—no matter what. It's true that the intimacy of your relationship with God can be broken by your unconfessed sin, but a broken relationship doesn't mean his love is gone.

You are unconditionally loved by God, who himself is love (1 John 4:8 states that God is love). He sees your every thought, word, and action, and he loves the ugly stuff as well as the good stuff. Gain courage from the assurance of his love. Don't dwell on the fear of disappointing him. When you sin, acknowledge it, confess it, repent, and move forward with the confidence of his unchanging love for you. Remember that he has a high goal for you: that your faith in him will grow deeper and stronger. In that growth, your dependence on him will be fueled by trust, and your service to him will be fueled by love.

32

Power from Vulnerability

He said to me, "My grace is sufficient for you, for my power is made perfect in weakness." Therefore I will boast all the more gladly about my weaknesses, so that Christ's power may rest on me.

2 CORINTHIANS 12:9

Letting others see your failures is one of the most difficult things to do. It's hard to be vulnerable with others. Sometimes it's even hard to be vulnerable with God. Do you struggle to ask him for help overcoming sins that you don't want to admit to him?

Guess what—you're not fooling God with your silent dishonesty. Here's what you need to understand: you don't have to be perfect to come to him. God's power is working in you, helping you in the areas where you're weak. It's okay that you need him—he wants you to need him. When God works in your life, giving you strength and victory, his power is evident to you as well as to others who know your struggles. Seeing his work in your life gives you, as well as those who are watching your life, courage to trust him more readily. Be bravely vulnerable with God. Ask him for help. Let his glory be revealed through you by the way he works in your heart and life.

33

Courage to Be Still

He says, "Be still, and know that I am God;
I will be exalted among the nations,
I will be exalted in the earth."

PSALM 46:10

What image does the phrase "be still" bring up in your mind? Sitting or lying down with no movement at all? Being completely silent? Neither of those things is easy to do, at least when you're awake. Why does God say to be still? Take a look at some of the possibilities:

Be still—Stop running around and doing, doing, doing. Just stop. Sit quietly in a place where you can center your thoughts on God.

Be quiet—Even as you think about God, don't start giving him a to-do list of all the problems you want him to solve. Think about his love for you. Think about his beautiful creation. Think about his power.

Be centered—Don't let your mind begin making lists of all the things you need to do once you're finished being still. Psalm 46:10 says, "Be still, and know that I am God," so keep your thoughts centered on who God is.

Why is being still important? Because stopping your activity, your list-making, and your requests gives you a chance to focus on who God is and to be refreshed in your relationship with him.

Do you have the courage to stop everything and be still? Doing so will bring great dividends in your relationship with Christ.

34

Courage to Share Your Life with Others

Rejoice with those who rejoice; mourn with those who mourn.

ROMANS 12:15

Do you have the courage to engage in someone else's life to the point that you share in their rejoicing or their mourning? Do you have the courage to allow others into your life at the same level? It's not easy. You have to be transparent and vulnerable. Is it important to share your life experiences with others? Scripture instructs you to share with those people God brings into your circle, and he gives wisdom as to which ones to be most open with. God does this because he knows that living in community is important. Being connected with others allows you to support one another through joys and sorrows. It helps everyone know they aren't alone in life. Friendships give strength and encouragement to keep going in the struggles you face, and it's just more fun to have people to celebrate your joys.

Ask God for the courage to be open to building community by sharing your life with others and engaging in their experiences too.

35

The Future

> "I know the plans I have for you," declares the LORD, "plans to prosper you and not to harm you, plans to give you hope and a future."
>
> JEREMIAH 29:11

Perhaps you are familiar with the phrase, "Upset the applecart." It refers to everything in life being turned upside down. It's scary when life takes a turn where a job is lost or a relationship ends. The future looks pretty confusing as you attempt to pick up the pieces of your life and move on. In fact, it takes real courage to turn your eyes to the future and move on from the rubble of the loss you've experienced.

The good news is that the plans for your future are not left to chance. You can take courage in the fact that every moment and every day of your life ahead is in God's hands. He has a plan for you, so any changes that have recently "upset the applecart" of your life did not take him by surprise. Trust him to navigate your path through those changes, to take you where he wants you to be. As you trust his plan and follow him, you will see his new plan develop, and it will be good. God loves you and wants good things for your future. So keep your heart focused on God as you turn your thoughts to what's next in your life. It will be good. He promised.

36

Courage to Love Yourself

I praise you because I am fearfully and wonderfully made;
your works are wonderful,
I know that full well.

PSALM 139:14

There used to be a saying floating around Christian circles: "God don't make no junk." The idea, of course, is that every person has worth because every person is created by God and made in his image. It goes right along with this lovely verse from Psalm 139.

The truth is that you are unique and wonderful. God made you the way he wants you to be. You are not like everyone else, and that's good. He gave you the personality you have. He gave you the talents you possess, the interests that pique your curiosity, your body type, your looks . . . he made you to be exactly you. Of course, you have the task of taking care of your body, your health, and your attitude. Keeping your heart focused on knowing and serving God is the foundation for doing that.

Don't let discouragement or struggles keep you from praising God for who you are. Push self-critical thoughts away and celebrate God's creativity that shows in you. Praise him for what you are learning about yourself, because the core of who you are is from God, and it is good.

37

You Matter to God

Are not two sparrows sold for a penny? Yet not one of them will fall to the ground outside your Father's care. And even the very hairs of your head are all numbered. So don't be afraid; you are worth more than many sparrows.

MATTHEW 10:29–31

Satan tries to make you doubt your value to God by saying you don't matter because you're not a "star" for God. Maybe you just wash the church nursery toys or take home the kitchen towels to throw in your own laundry. Maybe you don't teach a Bible study, but you do pick up a friend who doesn't drive so she can be a part of the study. You have many ways of serving, but Satan will try to convince you that no one notices and your service doesn't matter.

Sparrows are small, common birds. So how amazing is it that not even one falls to the ground without God knowing? Do you believe you are more important to God than even one sparrow? In fact, you're so important to him that he knows how many hairs are on your head, and that number changes daily!

Don't let Satan bury you in "I don't matter" thoughts. Call on God's power for the courage to push those thoughts away. Know that everything you do for God matters. There is no small service. You matter to him more than you could ever imagine!

38

Showing Kindness

> *Do not forget to show hospitality to strangers, for by so doing some people have shown hospitality to angels without knowing it.*
>
> HEBREWS 13:2

You are probably willing to help a family member or friend who needs something. You might even go out of your way to show kindness to a loved one. Are you also open to helping someone you don't know very well? Would you invite someone you don't know well to lunch? Would you sit by someone you don't know yet at a church dinner? What if by showing kindness to a stranger you are actually showing kindness to one of God's own angels, as this verse suggests?

The courage to show kindness to a stranger gives you the opportunity to show the honesty and depth of your love for God and to share his love for them. It's an exercise in loving-kindness.

If you find the thought of doing anything more than saying hello to a stranger terrifying, that's okay. You don't have to do it alone. Ask God to give you the courage you need. Ask him to direct your path toward those to whom you can show kindness. Be willing to step out of your comfort zone. God will use your kindness in amazing ways to bless others, and you will be blessed in the process!

39

Standing Bare before God

Test me, LORD, and try me,
examine my heart and my mind.

PSALM 26:2

Baring your soul before God happens only after you've allowed the Holy Spirit to convict you of whether you're living in obedience to him. Are you courageous enough to do both? Standing "naked" before God and yourself, with your thoughts and motives revealed, is humbling. Of course, nothing is hidden from God. He already knows your deepest thoughts and motives. So why does the psalmist make this request? Perhaps so that, as you echo these words, you also take an honest look at your heart and motives.

God convicts you and challenges you to be more obedient to his Word because his love for you is so deep that he wants you to be the best you possible. He knows you can love and encourage others. He knows you can serve him and grow his kingdom.

Facing the condition of your heart and mind right now could be difficult, depending on your circumstances, but being honest with yourself can move you to become more intimate in your relationship with God, and that is a wonderful blessing.

40

Never Alone

The Lord himself goes before you and will be with you; he will never leave you nor forsake you. Do not be afraid; do not be discouraged.

DEUTERONOMY 31:8

When you're going through a hard time and it seems to go on for a long while, there is a temptation to feel that you're all alone and no one understands what you're dealing with. If your struggles sink you into depression, friends and family may take a step back from you because they don't know how to help. Your aloneness makes your struggle even more discouraging. But you can gain courage from this promise in Deuteronomy that reminds you that you are never really alone. God promises to be with you always and nothing you do will cause him to turn away from you. God is your Creator and he guides each step of your life. He understands what you're struggling with. Not only does he understand your pain, he cares about your struggle.

When your struggles threaten to overtake your hope, remember God's love. You cannot even grasp how powerful God's love is for you. Allow yourself to see the ways, big and small, that he makes his presence known to you, even in your darkest times. Don't be afraid or discouraged. Stand tall and strong in God's presence, power, and love.

41

Controlling Yourself

Everyone should be quick to listen, slow to speak and slow to become angry, because human anger does not produce the righteousness that God desires.

JAMES 1:19–20

What's your behavior when you're annoyed, insulted, or angry? Are you pretty good at controlling yourself so that you don't angrily spout words that truly won't help a situation but that will definitely hurt others? Sometimes it's hard not to immediately jump to your own defense or judge someone else without having the full story.

Is your goal to reflect God's love to others so that they will want to know him too? Do you desire to honor and serve him by your words and actions? If these are your desires, your words and actions matter.

When a situation escalates and tempers flare, it takes strength to be quiet and let someone else say what they need to say rather than impulsively responding. You need strength to keep your anger from flaring up and to understand that your anger will not fix the situation or mend a relationship but will only make matters worse.

Having the courage to control your anger and hold off speaking until you know the whole story gives you the power to help defuse a situation and be the bearer of God's love to those around you.

42

Painful Times

God said, "Take your son, your only son, whom you love—
Isaac—and go to the region of Moriah. Sacrifice him there as
a burnt offering on a mountain I will show you."

GENESIS 22:2

God instructed Abraham to do the unthinkable—to sacrifice his own son to God. Abraham, with incredible faith and courage, obeyed. Abraham's obedience showed his complete submission to and trust in God. He was willing to give up something so very precious to him because God told him to.

Would you be able to obey such a command? Do you have the courage to trust God when his instructions are difficult or frightening? Can you trust him in the painful times of life?

Of course, you know the end of Abraham's story: once God saw Abraham's obedience, he stopped him from hurting Isaac, and he provided an animal for the sacrifice instead.

But God doesn't always stop terrible things from happening. He asks you to trust him with whatever comes into your life. He asks you to face it with courage because you trust him completely and you know that he can use any situation for his glory.

43

Prayer

> *Do not be anxious about anything, but in every situation, by prayer and petition, with thanksgiving, present your requests to God.*

PHILIPPIANS 4:6

Some people become defined by their anxiety because it's infused in everything in their lives. They worry not only about the crises they are facing but also about all the what-if scenarios their minds can imagine.

The problem with constant anxiety is that it saps your strength. Power, trust, and courage fade away as anxiety rules in your heart. Some people suffer from anxiety disorders, which are beyond their control. Thankfully, medication and counseling are available to help manage those conditions. But for those who choose to worry about things, God gives the antidote: prayer. Tell God what's weighing so heavily on your heart. Ask him to give you courage and strength to face your trials. Don't forget to thank him for what you're going to learn through the experience. Trust him to guide your steps, your thoughts, your words, and your actions.

Why will talking to God about your worries lessen your anxiety? Because spending time talking with him helps you remember that he loves you very much. He wants good things for you. He promises to hear your prayers and answer them. You can trust him.

44

Deep Thoughts

*May these words of my mouth and this meditation of
my heart
be pleasing in your sight,
Lord, my Rock and my Redeemer.*

Psalm 19:14

The words that come flying out of your mouth reflect the true condition of your heart. You can put on an outward appearance of kindness, concern, and gentleness toward others while your heart is cruel, selfish, and judgmental. You can fool others, but you can never fool God. And you don't fool yourself either.

Make these words in Psalm 19 your prayer. Ask the Lord to help you measure your words. There will be times when you need his discernment to know that you should be silent rather than reactive. There will be times when you need his strength to be courageous enough to walk away rather than speak unkindly.

God is your Rock and Redeemer. All you say and do represents him to others. Make it your goal to not only live in a way that is pleasing in his sight but also speak and relate to others in a way that pleases him. Allow him to be your teacher as you learn to love him and others more truly and deeply.

45

Stay Focused

I keep my eyes always on the LORD.
With him at my right hand, I will not be shaken.

PSALM 16:8

o you long for courage to grow in your heart? There's only one way that can happen and that is to keep your eyes focused on the Lord.

How do you stay focused on God? You do so by reading his Word every day and spending time thinking about what it says. He will speak into your heart through his words if you will be still and listen. Remember to talk with him and tell him what matters to you and where you need his help. You will see him answer your prayers, and that will encourage you to trust him more.

Where you focus your attention impacts the direction your heart takes. Make it your goal to keep your heart firmly focused on God so that nothing else becomes more important to you than he is. Focusing on his strength, power, and love will grow your courage to stand strong for him, to stay faithful to him, and to trust him more than anything or anyone else. Your strength comes only from God, so when you are focused on him, you have courage that is based on your confidence in him. Nothing can pull you away from his love.

46

Just Believe

Overhearing what they said, Jesus told him, "Don't be afraid; just believe."

MARK 5:36

When your worst fears come true, how strong is your faith? Do you trust that God is paying attention and that he cares about what you're going through?

Jairus asked Jesus to come to his house because his daughter was very sick. Jairus was afraid she would die, and he believed that Jesus could heal her. But before Jesus could go with the worried father, some of Jairus's servants came and told him that his daughter had already died. Don't you imagine that Jairus was heartbroken and even disappointed that Jesus hadn't hurried to his house? But—because the story is never over when Jesus is involved—Jesus said, "Don't be afraid; just believe." Maybe that was hard for Jairus, but he and Jesus went to his house and Jesus raised the dead little girl back to life! No doubt Jairus's trust in Jesus grew stronger, deeper, and more courageous because of Jesus's work there.

What would it take for your faith to grow stronger, deeper, and more courageous? If you have a crushing disappointment such as Jairus had, do you give Jesus a chance to show you his power through it? Your faith will grow stronger and more courageous as you see Jesus's work in your life.

In the Wilderness

See, I am doing a new thing!
 Now it springs up; do you not perceive it?
I am making a way in the wilderness
 and streams in the wasteland.

ISAIAH 43:19

If you've ever lost your job and searched and waited a very long time for a new one, you know how hopeless the future can appear. It feels like your online applications and sent résumés go into some black hole, never to be seen again. It's depressing. You can even identify with the Israelites who wandered in the wilderness for forty years. Forty years without really knowing where they were going. Just wandering.

Here's the thing: like the Israelites, even when you're in the wilderness for a long time, you're not out of God's mind. He knows what's happening to you. You aren't out of his control, and he does still have a plan for your future.

God is making a new way through the wilderness. He may not let you bypass it, but he will get you through that difficult time to a place of purpose and productivity again. So step boldly into the darkness of the wilderness. Step firmly onto the path he reveals, even if he shows you only one step at a time. Move forward with the courage that comes from the assurance that God is creating a new thing and opening a new way for your future!

48

Loving When It's Hard

Love each other deeply, because love covers over a multitude of sins.

1 PETER 4:8

ove is a powerful emotion. Truly loving someone helps you overlook hurts. After all, everyone messes up once in a while. Sometimes someone who loves you hurts you, often unintentionally. Because of love you take the time to understand why the situation happened. Love, as described in 1 Corinthians 13, is patient. Love doesn't hold grudges. Love isn't selfish. Love puts others before self. Sometimes that action takes courage—courage to place your emotions in the background and to understand what's going on in someone else's heart or life.

Love does that. It overlooks moments of pain and doesn't try to get revenge. Love wants the best for the other person, even if that means you don't get what you want. Love lifts; it doesn't oppress.

God's love for you is the perfect example of the power of love. Because of his love, your sins are forgiven. Because of his love, your shortcomings are overlooked. Because of his love, he provides ways for you to learn to love him better and to love others with his true love.

49

God-Honoring Conversation

*Even fools are thought wise if they keep silent,
and discerning if they hold their tongues.*

PROVERBS 17:28

When discussions get heated on subjects that you have strong feelings about, are you strong enough to be quiet? Why is it important that you hold your tongue in situations like this? Because such discussions often escalate into arguments that no one can win. Feelings are hurt and relationships are damaged. Being cautious about engaging in such arguments takes courage to resist stating your opinion.

What's more important than arguing your viewpoints is showing love to your friends and neighbors. Loving others is the second greatest commandment according to Jesus (see Matt. 22:39). While it's important to take a stand for scriptural truth, it's also important to do so with kindness and gentleness and the understanding that arguing seldom changes anyone's mind.

Keep silent and be thoughtful so that relationships stay strong. God will give you opportunities to share your beliefs and opinions in private so you can have meaningful discussions.

Ask the Lord to give you the courage and strength to hold your tongue and the opportunities to speak privately with those you are concerned about. Always keep the focus of your conversations on honoring God in all you say.

50

Courage to Stand Strong

The Spirit God gave us does not make us timid, but gives us power, love and self-discipline.

2 TIMOTHY 1:7

What does your faith in God mean to you? Think about what Jesus went through on this earth so that, through him, you could have the privilege of a personal relationship with God. Is your faith important enough to you to publicly show that you value his suffering, torture, and death? Or are you sometimes flippant about your relationship with God? Are you sometimes embarrassed to call yourself a Christian because someone might be cynical about the reality of God or about your need to have him in your life? The bottom-line question is, Does what Jesus did for you matter enough that you will take a public stand for him? Will you stand for him regardless of what others say or think?

There may be times when it is difficult or even dangerous to take a stand for God, but he does not intend for you to be timid about him. He will give you the power to stand for him. He will give you a love for him that overshadows all else and the self-discipline to courageously stand for him. You will be a witness to his power and love by your courage to declare your faith in him.

51

Your Shining Life

Let your light shine before others, that they may see your good deeds and glorify your Father in heaven.

MATTHEW 5:16

The only way people who don't know Jesus will learn about him is if someone tells them. Scripture repeatedly instructs believers to share their faith with others—to tell them of God's love and of what Jesus did so that they can have a personal relationship with God.

Does it frighten you to think about actually speaking about your faith? Are you fearful of not having the right words to explain your relationship with God? Are you concerned about how your efforts to share will be received by others?

The first step in sharing your faith is to let your light shine. You do that by living your life in a way that shows God is most important to you. Honor him with your life by obeying his commands. Share his love by showing kindness and respect to others. Give others the chance to see the depth of God's love for them through your love and through your shining life.

52

A Powerful Presence

You will receive power when the Holy Spirit comes on you; and you will be my witnesses in Jerusalem, and in all Judea and Samaria, and to the ends of the earth.

ACTS 1:8

Do you long to have real power in your life? Do you feel that you could be a better person, better spouse, better parent, better Christian if only you had power? You do have it—Jesus promised! You have the power of God's Holy Spirit to help you live in obedience to God's commands. He will give you guidance to recognize when you are being disobedient. The Spirit will spark your conscience to realize when you're making bad choices or when you could do better. He will convict you when you're living for yourself by putting your own desires before obeying God or helping others.

The Holy Spirit will guide you with the words you need to have in order to share the message of God's love and care with others. He will help you explain how important your own relationship with God is and how he has changed your life. He will use you to bring others to God.

The Holy Spirit is God's power residing in your heart. He will help you know how to pray, to live, and to speak. When you feel timid or afraid, remember his powerful, protecting, strengthening, loving presence is always with you.

53

Courageous Honesty

The LORD detests lying lips,
but he delights in people who are trustworthy.

PROVERBS 12:22

Honesty is very important, but is a little white lie really a big deal? Doesn't everyone pad the truth once in a while? Well, whether everyone pads the truth or not, God is not a fan of lying.

Sometimes it takes a great deal of courage to be honest and especially to be honest and kind at the same time. Being consistently honest shows your character. It lets others know they can trust you and depend on you.

While it's certainly important to be kind, it's also important to learn how to be honest in your kindness. Even little white lies can damage the trust others have in you. If you always say things like, "Yes, that song you sang was the best. You're the best singer ever!" regardless of what you feel is true, your friends will begin to not value your opinion because they won't be able to trust it.

As God's child, it is important to faithfully represent him to others by your trustworthiness and honesty. Honor God with your honesty and couch it in kindness. Be courageous enough to find a way to always tell the truth.

54

Coal or Diamonds

> *Blessed is the one who perseveres under trial because, having stood the test, that person will receive the crown of life that the Lord has promised to those who love him.*
>
> JAMES 1:12

Coal and diamonds both have the element of carbon in common. So what makes coal stay black and common while diamonds become beautiful and valuable? The answer: heat and pressure applied to the carbon while it's deep inside the earth.

Did you catch that? Pressure makes something wonderful out of something ordinary. Problems and pressure in your life can do the same thing if you let them. You will have problems in your life. There's no doubt about that. How you face them makes all the difference in whether they will change you for the better.

Scripture tells you that God is always with you. Nothing happens to you that he doesn't know about. He offers you strength and perseverance if you will trust him and depend on him to be the source of all you need. He asks you to trust that your difficulties and crises can draw you closer to him and strengthen your faith in him—the ultimate goal. He may not take away your problems, but he will not leave you to go through them alone. Life will bring problems, which will make you stronger and more dependent on God.

55

Courage to Try New Things

The LORD makes firm the steps
*   of the one who delights in him;*
though he may stumble, he will not fall,
*   for the LORD upholds him with his hand.*

PSALM 37:23–24

I t's relatively easy to be courageous when you know exactly what you're doing and how to do it. When you're repeating a task you've done dozens of times before, or when you have a mentor working step-by-step with you, there isn't much to fear.

How do you respond when the Lord presents you with a new challenge? What if he asks you to do something for which other people will be depending on you? Do you believe that if God asks you to do something, he will guide your steps and teach you the details of what you need to know? That he will strengthen you and give you wisdom? God will equip you and guide you if you will depend on him and trust him. He will not ask you to do something hoping that you'll fail! He wants you to succeed—for yourself and for his work.

Move forward with courage, knowing that God will uphold you if you stumble. He will honor your dependence on him and redeem any mistakes you make, using them for good.

56

God Asks You to Pray

Call to me and I will answer you and tell you great and unsearchable things you do not know.

Jeremiah 33:3

Prayer is the greatest privilege God has provided for his children. Just think about it—you can speak directly to the Creator of everything! You can go to the One who is in control of all, the One whose power and strength are unmatched, and pour out your heart. Tell him what you worry about, who you are concerned about, what you need his help with, and what you want him to do.

Never feel that your request is too small or too self-focused. If it's on your heart, God wants to know about it. You never need to feel that he doesn't want to listen to your prayers. God asks you to talk with him. He wants to hear, and he promises not only to listen but to answer! He may not always answer in the way you want him to, but that's because he sees a bigger picture of life than you do, and his goals for you are that you will have a stronger faith and a deeper trust in him.

Honestly talk to God. Tell him your fears, disappointments, and concerns, and believe that he is listening. Then look for his answers. He will show you great and wonderful things. He promises!

57

Getting Out of Your Comfort Zone

> *This is what the LORD Almighty said: "Administer true justice; show mercy and compassion to one another. Do not oppress the widow or the fatherless, the foreigner or the poor. Do not plot evil against each other."*
>
> ZECHARIAH 7:9–10

Some people are easy to care about. You like them, so you care if they are suffering with an illness or if they have a need for meals or financial help. There are some people you naturally want to help with things like yard work or transportation for appointments or errands. However, there are some people who are not easy to help. Perhaps they have different beliefs from yours, or they seem unapproachable, or you feel you don't have much in common with them.

Yet true justice is to show mercy and compassion to everyone, not just those like us. People who are different from you—those to whom it may be more of a stretch to show mercy and kindness—may be the ones who need it most. They may be the most alone and afraid. You can be the vehicle that brings God's love to them. Be courageous enough to care for those who take you outside your comfort zone. Ask God to open your eyes to those who need a kind word, a hot meal, a ride, or just a smile. Ask him to make you willing and ready to show his love to those who need it most. He will give you the courage as he gives you the opportunities.

58

Courage to Answer

The LORD came and stood there, calling as at the other times, "Samuel! Samuel!"

Then Samuel said, "Speak, for your servant is listening."

1 SAMUEL 3:10

Sometimes children are very choosy as to when they will respond to a parent's call. At times they choose to ignore the call until the parent's voice reaches a certain decibel level. Maybe they do this because they're afraid of being disciplined or given a chore to do. Whatever the reason, they may not answer until the situation is serious and by then, they could very well be in trouble.

What if Samuel had refused to answer God's call? What if, when God called "Samuel!" for the fourth time, the young boy had closed his eyes and pretended to be asleep? We might not be reading his story in the Bible then.

Well, what if God called your name? Would you have the courage to answer, "Speak, for your servant is listening"? Are you courageous enough to listen to what God has to say and then do what he asks you to do? Okay, maybe you won't hear God's audible voice, but he will speak to you through his Word. He will guide you, teach you, and challenge you. Will you listen? Will you answer? Will you respond?

59

Complete Trust

Trust in the LORD with all your heart
  and lean not on your own understanding;
in all your ways submit to him,
  and he will make your paths straight.

PROVERBS 3:5–6

Trusting God is a big part of building a relationship with him. Does it take courage to trust him? Yes, but even more than courage, trusting God is based on the understanding of how very much he loves you. Remember that God loves you so deeply that he sent his only Son to earth to teach about him and his love for you. Jesus then took the penalty for your sins on himself. He was tortured and killed to pay the price for your sins and make it possible for you to have a personal relationship with God. That was all done because of his love for you. You know that someone who loves you that much certainly wants only good things for you, which should make it easier for you to trust God.

Trusting God is very important, but don't miss two vital things in these verses from Proverbs. You read that you must trust God "with all your heart" and submit to him "in all your ways." You cannot trust God partway or submit only when you feel like it. Go all in with God and enjoy the blessings of his love and guidance.

60

Courage to Rejoice

Rejoice always, pray continually, give thanks in all circumstances; for this is God's will for you in Christ Jesus.

1 THESSALONIANS 5:16–18

Gratitude comes easily when things are going well in your life. However, even when we remember to thank God for his blessings in the good times, we may struggle with thanking him in the hard times.

It takes strength and courage to have an attitude of gratefulness when you're buried in pain and trouble—and yet God says to rejoice, no matter what's going on, and be thankful in every circumstance. Does he know how hard that is?

Of course he knows it's hard. It does take strength and courage to remain positive when you're hurting, but when you trust God and believe that he is in control, no matter what is happening, you have the courage to rejoice in the hard times. You recognize that God is teaching you through the struggles you have and, in fact, they draw you closer to him. So even in hard times you can rejoice and be grateful!

61

Controlling Your Thought Life

Finally, brothers and sisters, whatever is true, whatever is noble, whatever is right, whatever is pure, whatever is lovely, whatever is admirable—if anything is excellent or praiseworthy—think about such things.

PHILIPPIANS 4:8

You know what happens when you have a big, beautiful basket of fruit that looks so very delicious, but buried in the middle of the basket is a piece of rotten fruit. If you don't take it out, it spreads its decay to any other fruit that's touching it. What began as one small bad spot can destroy much of the good fruit.

Your thought life can be that way. One small negative or critical thought can spread throughout your attitude if you do not courageously, intentionally pluck it out.

Intentionally pushing aside thoughts that do not honor God and others is done by replacing them with healthier thoughts. Focus your mind on the truth of Scripture. Fill your mind with the encouragement of God's love for you and the reminders of his patience and forgiveness.

Sometimes you may need God's help to see beyond the negativity of the present moment. Ask him to help you notice the evidence of his presence, protection, and love in each situation and in each person with whom you have contact. Remember his past work in your life to be reminded of his love in the present. Think on those things.

62

Growing in Godliness

Physical training is of some value, but godliness has value for all things, holding promise for both the present life and the life to come.

1 TIMOTHY 4:8

Learning to be godly means learning to think, feel, and behave more like God than like a person who doesn't know him at all. Does this happen easily? No, it doesn't. That's why it takes courage to commit to learning and growing toward godliness. The effort to grow more godly improves your life here on earth as well as the lives of those around you. Godliness goes even beyond your earthly life because as you live for God you also lay up treasures in heaven.

Think about how you strengthen and train your body's muscles. The only way to do so is by exercising them over and over to make them stronger. You have to be intentional, consistent, and persistent. You have to accept that your muscles will get tired and sore as they grow stronger.

Training for godliness also takes intentionality, consistency, and persistence. These characteristics are applied to the acts of studying God's Word each day, praying, and asking for his help. Growing closer to God often comes only through pain and suffering, so be ready! Realize that the privilege of knowing God and growing to be like him is worth whatever comes.

63

Courage to Praise

Let everything that has breath praise the Lord.
Praise the Lord.

PSALM 150:6

It shouldn't take courage to praise the Lord. But in a culture that's critical of God and anything related to him, you may sometimes need to summon courage for the simple act of praising God.

It's an interesting dilemma because praising God is a wonderful experience, so of course it's something you want to do. Praising God lifts your spirits and reminds you of the many blessings he showers on you. Praise reminds you of his power, strength, and love. God tells you to praise him. In fact, as this verse says, everything that breathes should praise the Lord.

Praising God with your words and attitudes tells other people how important he is to you. Your praise helps others learn about him and how strong, powerful, creative, and loving he is. Publicly praising God is a witness to others.

Praising God is also a witness to you because it helps you overcome discouragement and doubts. As you spend time mentioning his blessings, his gifts, and the times he has helped or protected you, you and others will see his love.

Ask God for the courage to openly praise him and to share your praise with anyone around you. Make praise your witness!

64

A New You

I will give you a new heart and put a new spirit in you; I will remove from you your heart of stone and give you a heart of flesh.

EZEKIEL 36:26

Who were you before you asked God into your life? If you were rebellious, dishonest, or not very nice, you may find it hard to forgive yourself for things you did or said. It's difficult to move forward in your new life if you're holding on to the old one out of guilt.

Here's the good news: no matter what kind of person you were before—rebellious, cynical, abusive, unkind—it doesn't matter. God will change you from the inside out by changing your heart. Your hardened heart, which keeps you at a distance from him, will be softened to be caring, considerate, compassionate, and loving. That's God's influence in your life. He sees the person you can be when he is in your life.

Don't give up on yourself. Believe that God can—and will—change your heart to help you become more like him. All you have to do is be willing to let him teach you, guide you, and give you that new spirit and caring heart.

65

Never Changing

Jesus Christ is the same yesterday and today and forever.
HEBREWS 13:8

In our world, things change at lightning speed. Technology is outdated as soon as you learn it. Friends may move away or fade from your life. Jobs disappear. Where can you put your confidence and trust?

There's only one Person and situation you can trust to never change, and that is Jesus and his love for you. You can always trust his love because many times in Scripture he promises his constant, unconditional, forgiving love. You can also trust that the standards and commandments of obedience to God that Jesus taught will never change. What was right hundreds of years ago is still right today. Jesus promised to always be with you, no matter what. Nothing can change that. Nothing can separate you from his incredible love.

Step courageously into your life in Jesus, knowing that you can depend on the fact that he is still the same Jesus you meet in Scripture. You can trust that he longs to know and forgive you and that he longs for your love for him and your faith in him to grow deeper.

66

In the Tough Times

I know what it is to be in need, and I know what it is to have plenty. I have learned the secret of being content in any and every situation, whether well fed or hungry, whether living in plenty or in want.

PHILIPPIANS 4:12

Praising God in the sunshine is easy. Praising God in the storm—not so much. When life is good, when everyone is healthy, when your job is successful—well, if you take time to actually think about it—of course you feel thankful and perhaps even verbalize your thanks to God.

Why does it take courage to praise God when life is hard, when you face health struggles, or when your job is taken away? Even beyond your own struggle to really praise God during these times, others may question what you have to praise God for or where your God is when you're struggling against so many negatives.

Praising in the hard times may be difficult, but that is when your trust in God is most obvious to yourself and others and when it is truly the most real. You can praise in the difficult times as well as the wonderful times because you know that God is always with you. Believe and trust that his love and strength will see you through whatever comes.

Praise God with courage and boldness, whatever your circumstance may be. Your praise becomes your testimony of his faithfulness.

67

No Fear

When I am afraid, I put my trust in you.
In God, whose word I praise—
in God I trust and am not afraid.
What can mere mortals do to me?

PSALM 56:3–4

Where do you turn when you're scared? Where do you find comfort? There can be some temptation to turn to food, money, friends, success, yourself, or a multitude of other things, when the only true solution to your fear is God.

Trust God. His Word proclaims his strength and power. Nothing and no one is greater than he is. Not others who judge or criticize you. Not your anxiety about your job and what your future might be. Not your fears about things that are happening in the world.

His Word also promises that there is nothing that can separate you from his love. That means you have no reason to fear any person or any situation. God's power, knowledge, and strength can take on anything you face. And he will take it on because he loves you even more than you can possibly imagine.

When you're afraid, spend time reading God's Word. It will remind you of God's presence, power, and love.

68

Work to Do

> *Have I not commanded you? Be strong and courageous. Do not be afraid; do not be discouraged, for the LORD your God will be with you wherever you go.*
>
> JOSHUA 1:9

God gives you opportunities to do different jobs for him throughout your lifetime. You may feel confident about doing some of the work. But some tasks may frighten you because they seem bigger than life, they're too difficult, they demand too much responsibility, or you feel untrained and unprepared for them.

It's okay that you have these anxious feelings as long as you don't stay there. When a job seems too difficult or a responsibility seems overwhelming, turn to God for help. He gave you the work to do, and he will make certain that you have what you need to accomplish it. Tell him you're overwhelmed or unprepared. Ask him for the knowledge, discernment, and skill to not only do the work but do it well.

Then enter into the job knowing that God is with you each step of the way. When you need knowledge, he will supply it or he will bring someone alongside you who can help you.

Be strong and courageous because your God has work for you, and he will make sure you are prepared to do it. Lean on him. Listen to him. Trust him.

69

Nothing in Return

God demonstrates his own love for us in this: While we were still sinners, Christ died for us.

ROMANS 5:8

What does it take for you to forgive someone who has hurt you? Is it necessary for them to repent and apologize for their behavior? Can you forgive them even if they give no indication that they are sorry for hurting you?

It is hard to forgive when you've been hurt, especially when it's by the actions of someone you love. But your example to follow is Jesus himself. He paid the ultimate price of giving his own life as the sacrifice to pay for your sins. He did that regardless of whether you would ever acknowledge or be sorry for your sin. He sacrificed because of his depth of love for you. He didn't demand anything from you before he did this. His love was enough.

Refusing to forgive another person until you get what you feel you deserve is a very human emotion. However, the goal in following Christ is to learn from his example. Be willing to let go of what you think you deserve and simply love and forgive without expecting anything in return. You will make your own heart healthier, and you will be showing a true example of God's love.

70

On Guard

Be on your guard; stand firm in the faith; be courageous; be strong. Do everything in love.

1 CORINTHIANS 16:13–14

Maybe you know this feeling: Something doesn't seem right, and you start feeling nervous, on edge. Your skin even feels prickly. Every sound reverberates in your mind. Every movement catches your eye. You are on guard because something is going to happen and you are prepared to face it.

Scripture tells you to be on guard where your faith is concerned. Pay attention to the temptations that try to pull you away from closeness with God. There will be times when Satan tries to direct you into focusing on yourself or having a critical spirit or, well, any of a myriad of behaviors that are disobedient to God's commands. Satan works so subtly that you may not realize your behavior is changing.

That's why you must be on guard. Stay in the Word. Listen to the Spirit's promptings in your heart. Be courageous and strong in asking Jesus to help you fight temptation. Know that God loves you very much and he will be your strength and help. Stand strong in your faith because of your love for him.

71

Courage to Honor God

Whether you eat or drink or whatever you do, do it all for the glory of God.

There's a wonderful illustration of this verse in the first chapter of the book of Daniel. Young Daniel and his friends were captives being trained to serve in the king's palace. They were strong, intelligent fellows who caught the eye of the official in charge. He put them in a special training program to serve the king. That meant they got better treatment and better food than the other captives. You might think that Daniel would be a fool to give up this elevated position, that he would be foolish to risk offending the official or the king. But he did.

Daniel knew that the food he and his friends were served had first been offered to idols. Because Daniel loved and served God, he believed it was wrong to eat it. So he courageously made a deal with the official. He and his friends were given only vegetables and water for ten days while the other young men ate the king's food. If he and his friends weren't the strongest and healthiest of all after the ten days, then they would eat the king's food. God honored Daniel's courage and he and his friends were the strongest of all!

Is there a stand you should make to show that your faith in God and your desire to honor him are the most important things to you? Do you have the courage to make that stand? God will honor your bravery.

72

The Only Salvation

Salvation is found in no one else, for there is no other name under heaven given to mankind by which we must be saved.

ACTS 4:12

Daniel 3 tells the story of three young men who believed that their salvation came from God and who chose to honor him. King Nebuchadnezzar commanded everyone to bow down to a gold statue he had made, but Shadrach, Meshach, and Abednego refused, declaring that they bowed only before God. The king wasn't happy about that. He offered them another chance to obey, and their refusal would mean they would be tossed into a blazing furnace. These three God followers didn't hesitate; again they declared they would bow only to God. They believed God would protect them if they went into the furnace.

What did Shadrach, Meshach, and Abednego expect to happen? Would God pour water in the furnace to put out the fire? Would he change the king's mind? Would he whisk them away?

God didn't do any of those things. The boys were tossed into a furnace so hot that the soldiers who threw them in were killed. But God honored their faith. An angel of God came into the furnace with them. They weren't burned— they didn't even smell like smoke when the amazed king called them out.

Shadrach, Meshach, and Abednego had the courage to face the fire, and God honored that faith. Do you need to choose to trust God rather than follow someone who wants you to turn away from him? Be courageous enough to honor God, and then be amazed at how he honors you.

73

Courage When Things Look Hopeless

He is the living God
and he endures forever;
his kingdom will not be destroyed,
his dominion will never end.
He rescues and he saves;
he performs signs and wonders
in the heavens and on the earth.
He has rescued Daniel
from the power of the lions.

DANIEL 6:26–27

When you diligently obey God and stand up for him, do you expect him to protect you from problems? Consider Daniel. He loved and obeyed God. He took a stand of obedience to God early in his life and continued it throughout his life. Daniel valued his prayer life—his personal communication with God. So even when his enemies got the king to decree that no one could pray to anyone but him, Daniel continued praying to God, and he didn't try to hide it.

Daniel's choice to honor God resulted in his being tossed into a den of lions. God didn't protect Daniel from the prescribed punishment; however, God did protect Daniel from the lions. He honored Daniel's obedience, just not in the way Daniel may have expected.

Do you have the courage to honor God, even when you face persecution, whether it comes through sarcasm, humiliation, or physical danger? Do you trust God to protect you because of your obedience? Are you willing to accept the form his protection takes, even if it isn't what you hoped for? He does know what's happening, and he loves you and has a plan. Trust him.

74

Brave Changes

Don't urge me to leave you or to turn back from you. Where you go I will go, and where you stay I will stay. Your people will be my people and your God my God.

RUTH 1:16

When life as you know it seems to fall apart, do you have the courage to start over? God may turn your life in a completely new direction, which could draw you closer to him—but it could also be frightening. It could mean leaving everything that's familiar behind.

Consider Ruth. It seemed that her life was set—be a wife, have a family, grow old. Then her husband died, and everything changed. She could have gone home to her parents, but Ruth had seen something in the life of her mother-in-law, Naomi, that she was drawn to—Naomi's faith in God. When Naomi decided to return to her homeland, Ruth chose to go with her. She left behind everything that was familiar, including the faith of her childhood and family. The way her mother-in-law lived her life attracted Ruth to God, and she wanted him in her life. Ruth had the courage to make a change, and that courage gave her a new life and a new faith.

Life changes are stressful. It's difficult to adjust to new places and situations. Having the courage to follow when God leads you to new things offers growth in your faith and ministry for him. Be courageous and experience new things!

75

According to His Will

This is the confidence we have in approaching God: that if we ask anything according to his will, he hears us.

1 JOHN 5:14

Have you ever so desperately wanted God to do something for you that you literally cried out to him, begging him for action? Crying out is not a subdued, silent prayer but a tear-filled, passionate, breathless cry for his attention, care, and work.

Hannah did that. In 1 Samuel, chapter 1, we read that Hannah wanted more than anything to have a baby. She wanted a child so desperately that she fell to the ground and cried out to God for the blessing of motherhood. She cried aloud, not caring who heard her.

Sometimes we box prayers in by feeling that they need to be quiet and humble in order for us to show how much trust and submission are behind them. Some feel that if they cry out with passion, it may appear that they aren't happy with what God is doing.

It's okay to cry out to God with passion. Tell him what you want! Your cries do not mean you don't trust him or that you won't accept it if he does something different. He wants to know the passion in your heart. You can verbalize it to him. Then ask for the strength to accept whatever comes. As Jesus prayed: "Not my will, but yours" (Luke 22:42).

76

Brown Sugar Giving

> *Give, and it will be given to you. A good measure, pressed down, shaken together and running over, will be poured into your lap. For with the measure you use, it will be measured to you.*
>
> LUKE 6:38

Who doesn't love a freshly baked chocolate chip cookie? Warm, right from the oven, with soft, gooey chocolate chips—yum! If you are a baker, you know that a necessary ingredient in these sweet treats is brown sugar. Measuring brown sugar for your recipe is different from measuring other ingredients. Brown sugar is measured by packing it down into the measuring cup and pressing it firmly, so it seems that you're putting in twice as much as the recipe calls for.

Think about that kind of measurement as you consider giving, sharing, and encouraging and loving others. Step out of your comfort zone if necessary, and give until you think you can't give anymore. Give until it's obvious to all that your love for others is overflowing. Give of your time, energy, funds, and talents from the generosity of your heart. Even if no one gives you a pat on the back and you feel like no one notices, you can be sure that God notices. He sees the brown sugar sacrificial giving flowing from your heart, and you will be blessed for it.

77

Trusting God to Provide

Do not worry, saying, "What shall we eat?" or "What shall we drink?" or "What shall we wear?" For the pagans run after all these things, and your heavenly Father knows that you need them.

MATTHEW 6:31–32

Believing God will provide in a situation that appears to be hopeless is courageous faith. The widow who is described in 2 Kings 4 was in a desperate situation. After her husband's death, his creditor came after her. She had no money, so the man threatened to take her sons as slaves to pay the debt. When she asked Elisha for help, he asked what she had in the house. All she had was a jar of oil. He told her to send her sons to gather pots from the neighbors and fill them with the oil. She did, and the jar of oil did not run out until the last pot was filled. What an amazing story! We don't know for certain if the woman sold the oil as Elisha told her to do. But we can assume she obeyed the man of God and sold the oil to pay the creditor.

If so, she was saved from a hopeless situation. Where is the courage in her story? She did what Elisha—a man of God—told her to do, even though it could have made her look foolish to her sons and her neighbors.

No situation is hopeless when God is involved. Pull from the depth of your faith to trust him to work through whatever you're facing, and wait in strength and courage to see how he will save you.

78

Waiting for God's Timing

Be patient, then, brothers and sisters, until the Lord's coming.
See how the farmer waits for the land to yield its valuable crop,
patiently waiting for the autumn and spring rains.

JAMES 5:7

*L*ife brings various seasons as relationships, health, careers, and situations ebb and flow. Some things are wonderful, joy-filled blessings. Some are difficult and painful. It's important to have the courage to be patient during all seasons of life, and the comparison to nature in this verse reminds us of that. When a seed is planted in the ground, a plant does not immediately pop up. There are no flowers, no tomatoes on the vine, right away. The farmer must wait for the seed to respond to water, nutrients in the soil, and sunlight. Farming takes patience.

When the seasons of life bring difficult times, have the courage to wait. See how God grows your faith and teaches you to trust more deeply in him through the ways he brings water, nutrients, and sunlight into your situation. You will see that your courageous patience is rewarded in your walk with God, just as the farmer's patience is rewarded with the long anticipated crop. Good things come, even from hard times and even when we must wait.

79

It's Not Over

If we confess our sins, he is faithful and just and will forgive us our sins and purify us from all unrighteousness.

1 John 1:9

God graciously forgives our failures when we ask because he sees whether our heart truly desires to obey him.

The book of 2 Samuel tells of King David's affair with Bathsheba, who was another man's wife. Bathsheba became pregnant as a result of the affair. David tried to cover up the affair by bringing her husband home from the war, assuming husband and wife would sleep together. When that didn't happen, he had the man sent to the front lines of the war so he would be killed. David put a lot of work into covering up the first sin in this domino effect, yet God still referred to David as a man after God's own heart. Why? What did God see that no one else saw?

God saw deep into David's heart, which showed that even though he sinned and made bad choices, David was sorry for what he had done. He loved God and God's Word, he was repentant, and he was thankful for the renewal of forgiveness and second chances. David made the most of his second chance by honoring and praising God.

Maybe you've messed up big-time in your life. Maybe you feel that what you've done is unforgivable and that you are now damaged goods, so you could never serve God. That's not true. Believe in God's forgiveness and in the second chances he gladly gives. Maybe your story was changed by your sin and bad choices, but it isn't hopeless. Learn from David—your story is not over. God forgives. He looks at your heart.

80

Eternally Alive

Jesus said to her, "I am the resurrection and the life. The one who believes in me will live, even though they die; and whoever lives by believing in me will never die. Do you believe this?"

John 11:25–26

When Lazarus, the brother of Mary and Martha, died, the faith of his sisters was put to the test. Jesus was their good friend. They knew he could heal their brother, so they sent for him, but he didn't come until it was too late. When he arrived, Martha said, "Lord, . . . if you had been here, my brother would not have died" (John 11:21). It almost sounds like she blamed him for her brother's death because he didn't hurry to their sides.

Jesus's response to Martha was simply that she should believe. He is the resurrection and the life. He promises that all who believe in him will never die. Martha just needed to believe. You may know the rest of the story: Jesus called Lazarus from the grave back to life—for a while, at least.

Do you have the courage to believe when your heart is breaking from the loss of a loved one? Will Jesus call your loved one back to earthly life? Probably not. But he promised eternal life to those who have accepted him as their Savior, so when they close their eyes on earth, they open their eyes in heaven. Forever alive with Jesus. He promised.

81

Jumping out of the Boat

I can do all this through him who gives me strength.
PHILIPPIANS 4:13

Peter . . . impetuous, passionate risk taker. When Peter believed something, he was in 100 percent, and he didn't much care what anyone else thought. He believed Jesus's love, power, and strength were his, so when he saw Jesus walking toward the disciples' boat one day—on top of the water—he called out, "If it's you, . . . tell me to come to you on the water" (Matt. 14:28). Jesus told him to come, so Peter leaped out of the boat and started walking toward Jesus—ON TOP of the water! That was Peter. When he wanted something, he had the courage to go for it. When his focus on Jesus wavered, he sank. But Jesus saved him!

How's your courage? You may know the old saying, "If you keep on doing what you do, you'll keep on getting what you've got." If you want something new and exciting in your life, you must be willing to "get out of the boat." It can be pretty frightening, but you will never know the possibilities if you don't take the risk. Having the courage to take a chance opens the door for Jesus to show you new pathways in your life.

82

The Power of Change

The LORD is my strength and my shield;
my heart trusts in him, and he helps me.

PSALM 28:7

All the believers knew about Saul. Acts 8:3 reads, "Saul began to destroy the church. Going from house to house, he dragged off both men and women and put them in prison." Saul was known for persecuting believers. Christians were scared of him, so when God told Ananias, "Go to the house of Judas on Straight Street and ask for a man from Tarsus named Saul, for he is praying" (Acts 9:11), Ananias questioned the wisdom of that command. That's understandable because Ananias didn't yet know that Saul had met Jesus and was a changed man. But, to Ananias's credit, when God said, "Go," he went. He courageously trusted that Saul could change from the dangerous man he had been to a servant of God.

Do you believe that people can change 100 percent once Jesus comes into their hearts? If God told you to spend some time with someone who had been very far away from him and whose lifestyle and morals were completely the opposite of yours, would you have the courage to obey?

God can save anyone and completely rehab a heart that has been against him. If God gives you the opportunity to be a part of someone's new life for him, as he did with Ananias and Saul, be courageous and take the chance!

83

Courage to Obey

This is how we know that we love the children of God: by loving God and carrying out his commands.

1 JOHN 5:2

There may be times when God asks you to do something that makes absolutely no sense to you. That's what happened to Noah when God told him to build a boat . . . a very big boat. There was no reason for Noah to build a boat that big when no large body of water was close by. His friends thought he was a little crazy when he started working on it, but Noah obeyed God no matter what.

Noah had the courage to do what God asked, even when he saw no reason for it and he had to endure the comments of friends.

God does not always tell you the *why* of what he asks of you or the reason for circumstances that come into your life.

He asks you to trust him completely and to have the courage to obey and follow him, even when you can't see the *why*. Are you willing to step into darkness, trusting that your foot will land on something solid, even when you can't see it? Put your faith into courageous action.

84

Greatest Faith

When Jesus heard this, he was amazed at him, and turning to the crowd following him, he said, "I tell you, I have not found such great faith even in Israel."

How would you like to be the person Jesus referred to when he said he had never found such great faith before? It would be quite an honor, wouldn't it? The military officer to whom Jesus was referring had a servant whom he really cared about—the man was either a good servant or had become a friend. When the servant became very ill, the officer knew that Jesus could help. What's so amazing about this man's faith was that he believed Jesus could heal his servant without even coming to him. He knew that all Jesus needed to do was speak words of healing. The officer didn't have to be with his servant and see the healing in order to know it happened. He trusted Jesus that much.

Faith that doesn't have to see is courageous. Having faith that deep means that you believe God is working and answering your prayers. That you trust his timing and his choices in regard to what is best for all involved. It's not easy to always be courageous, but it's something to aspire to. Trust God so completely and be so convinced of his love that you believe in his answers before they are actually seen.

85

Courage to Face My Sin

I do not do the good I want to do, but the evil I do not want to do—this I keep on doing. Now if I do what I do not want to do, it is no longer I who do it, but it is sin living in me that does it.

ROMANS 7:19–20

Wouldn't it be nice if you could rewind life an hour or so at a time so you could do a little better? You know, respond with more kindness to a situation, be a bit more patient, listen more than talk, be generous without resentment . . . there are a multitude of things you might want to change if you got a do-over.

The easy way out is to blame your less-than-perfect behavior on someone or something else. But while someone or something else may have played into your words and actions, the bottom-line reason for them is sin. When sin has a foothold in your heart, it controls what you do, even when you don't really want to do it.

Be courageous—admit that you *do* sin instead of blaming other factors for your behavior. Ask the Lord to help you overcome sin in your life so you can grow to be more like Jesus. Remember that the Christian life is a journey and that you're always learning and growing.

86

Courage to Be You

We are God's handiwork, created in Christ Jesus to do good works, which God prepared in advance for us to do.

EPHESIANS 2:10

Self-esteem is an interesting topic to think about. You don't want to have so much self-esteem that it becomes pride, which leaves God out of consideration, but you should have enough self-esteem to be confident in who God made you to be.

This verse from Ephesians says that we are God's handiwork. Other Bible versions call us his masterpiece—the best of his work. Each person is created with unique talents, gifts, and personalities. In other words, God made you exactly the way he wants you to be. He doesn't want you to get stuck in the trap of comparing yourself to another person, wondering if you should be more like them. He wants you to be you. In fact, he doesn't just *want* you to be you, he *needs* you to be you. When each person is being who he made them to be and doing what he made them to do, all the parts of his kingdom fit together like a well-oiled machine.

Don't get caught in the trap of feeling you must be who the world says you should be. Have the courage to push aside what others think, and believe that you are special because of who God says you are and because of the way he made you.

87

Courage That Makes You Creative

By this everyone will know that you are my disciples, if you love one another.

JOHN 13:35

What a blessing friendship is. Sharing life with good friends makes life so much better. Are you the kind of person who would go out of your way to help your friends?

The men in Luke 5 went out of their way to help a sick friend. They got creative in order to bring the paralyzed man to Jesus and ask for healing for him. They carried their friend to the house where Jesus was teaching, but they couldn't get through the crowd of people there. That's when they got creative and took a chance. They tore a hole in the roof of the house and lowered the man down in front of Jesus. Would Jesus chastise them for disrupting his teaching? Would the homeowner be upset that they made a hole in the roof?

Would others who were waiting for Jesus's attention be upset that these men pushed their way ahead of them? The men didn't care. They were courageously creative in order to help their friend.

The only response to their actions that we know of is that of Jesus. He saw their faith as well as the sick man's faith, and he healed the man.

Are you courageously creative when it comes to helping others? Will you go out of your way to do so? Are you willing to be inconvenienced? Are you willing to be the kind of friend that you would like to have?

88

Greatest Commandments

"Love the Lord your God with all your heart and with all your soul and with all your strength and with all your mind"; and, "Love your neighbor as yourself."

LUKE 10:27

The hard part of obeying these two greatest commandments that Jesus gave is getting yourself out of the way. This verse challenges you to love God more than anything or anyone else—even yourself. Loving God as fully as this verse describes means completely trusting him with your life and willingly submitting your desires to him. It means giving all your thoughts, actions, and emotions over to him, and believing that what he chooses to bring into your life is all for your good. Understand that even if painful struggles come, they provide the opportunity to trust God more deeply and to grow closer to him.

The second commandment given here is to love your neighbor as yourself. What does that mean to you? It's actually more than what you may think at first. Loving another as you love yourself is actually loving another *more* than you love yourself. It's difficult to have the best interests of two people at the forefront of your mind. Putting others above yourself may not be easy, but doing so will show Jesus's love to others and draw you closer to God.

89

Guard Your Heart

Above all else, guard your heart,
for everything you do flows from it.
PROVERBS 4:23

Sin is sneaky. Satan is subtle. Each can slip into your life in such tiny ways that you may not even notice the changes in your actions and attitudes. It may happen so gradually that the sinful things slowly become habits that you're comfortable with, so they don't feel like sin.

Why does this Bible verse tell you to guard your heart? Possibly because sin often begins with a yearning, something you want to have or do. It may also start with the feeling that you deserve something or have been wronged in some way. If your heart isn't submitted to God and focused on obeying, serving, and reflecting him to others, those negative feelings will take root and grow into full-fledged sin.

How do you guard your heart? It's best to do so by asking God to hold you accountable for your thoughts and feelings. Ask him to reveal the beginning of sinful thoughts that might be running through your heart, and then ask him to give you the courage and strength to push them aside before they take root.

90

A Step at a Time

If my people, who are called by my name, will humble them-
selves and pray and seek my face and turn from their wicked
ways, then I will hear from heaven, and I will forgive their sin
and will heal their land.

2 Chronicles 7:14

What does this verse say to you? What do you hear God asking of his people? He's asking you to allow him to be the most important Person in your life. He's asking you to submit to him by giving up control of your life and following him. Is this scary? Well, it could be if you don't honestly trust that God loves you intensely and unconditionally and therefore has your best interests in mind.

To get to the point of trusting God in your relationship with him, you must get yourself out of the way. Stop trying to control your life. Submit to God's plan. Follow him even if you can't see the end result of his plan yet. Learn that you can trust him because he sees the big picture of your entire life and the role you play in his work on this earth.

Your courage may come one step at a time by trusting God in a small instance and, after seeing his love and care for you, knowing you can trust him in something bigger. Give yourself permission to grow in courage and trust, a step at a time, and learn to fully submit to him.

Carolyn Larsen is the bestselling author of more than fifty books for children and adults. She has been a speaker for women's events and classes around the world, bringing scriptural messages filled with humor and tenderness. For more information, visit carolynlarsen.com and follow her on Facebook.

Connect with
Carolyn

Author Photo: Bennorth Images of St. Charles, IL

CAROLYNLARSEN.COM

Carolyn Larsen

Rest in *God's Embrace*

words of
peace
for
Women

Carolyn Larsen

A 90-day devotional that will help you
remember God's presence in your days and see
your world from a positive perspective.

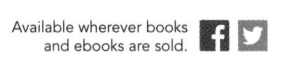

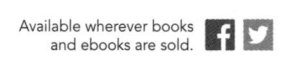

Find *Hope* through the Promises in God's Word

words of hope
for
Women

Carolyn Larsen

A 90-day devotional that will remind you that God has a plan and a purpose in everything—even the hard stuff—and you can trust him to keep his promises.

 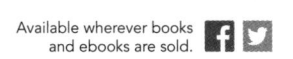